The Pillars of Intimacy

The Untold Tale of An Amazing Union

Francis J. Clifton

Chapter 1

Marriage

Chapter 2

Intimacy

Chapter 3

The Pillars of Intimacy

Chapter 4

Emotional Intimacy

Chapter 5

Financial intimacy

Chapter 6

Physical Intimacy

Chapter 7

Spiritual Intimacy

Chapter 8

Recreational Intimacy

Chapter 9

Sexual Intimacy

Chapter 10

Mental Intimacy

Chapter 11

Each Pillar Matters

Chapter 1

Marriage

Exactly when we first go completely gaga we regularly offer expressions like, "I love you" or "I want to go with you." The accentuation is on the "I" part of the circumstance. This is fine and normal. Regardless, certified sentiment in a sound marriage is based on tending to the prerequisites of our mate and not pretentiously in isolation.

It is just the beginning to Turn out to be irredeemably fascinated. It's the main stage in an amazing trip where two people become one. Anyway, the preposterous vibes of intimacy initially felt will dial down.

So how should a couple keep energy-fire-consuming? Being gallant and caring are two things they can do to light the flares. Actions speak louder than words. So your approach to acting towards your life partner should pass the sum of the singular method on to you (and this is the definitively accurate thing it does because it reveals how much or how negligible you genuinely care for them).

We are careful that veneration and captivation are two by and large various things. We also understand that reverence isn't just a tendency. Love is a decision — an obligation. It's the action of deliberately choosing to commit yourself and your energies to making your esteemed one happy.

In case your fondness is laid out upon opinions alone, your marriage will break down. The consideration should be on supporting the relationship and fostering an appreciation for one another every day. This prompts concordance and warmth. Likewise, you will begin experiencing direct what it genuinely means to cherish one another.

It is for this very reason that marriage urges consistently focuses on being careful towards one's accessories. Anyway, bias drags in and gags the relationship.

Love is more than a tendency - it's an activity word, a movement — that we show unendingly paying little brain to how we wind up feeling on some irregular day.

How conciliatory is your veneration? What could your mate say concerning the charitableness of your love? Is it valid or not that you are more enthused about what you can get away from the relationship or what you can put into the relationship?

Esteeming your mate conciliatorily and unselfishly makes authentic sentiment in marriage.

Chapter 2

Intimacy

What is intimacy? What is going on with intimacy? To a great extent people will do anything to gravitate toward someone they see as captivating, intriguing, or by and largely convincing. Is that being private?

Now and again singles will do essentially anything to gravitate toward someone they consider to be interesting, enrapturing, or inside and out overwhelming. One single woman I know goes through Starbucks every day to get her part of caffeine. One morning as she pushed toward the speaker to organize, she saw that the man in the truck before her looked very engaging. She took a gander at him through his back view reflect. Astounding! Alluring! Well ... I continue to ponder whether he's single. In a short second, she made a plan.

"Hey. Welcome to Starbucks. What could I anytime start for you today?"

"Well to start, might you anytime at some point work on something for me? Will you ask with regards to whether he's available?"

"You mean the individual in the truck? Suuuuuure. I'd a lot of need to. By what other means might I anytime at some point help you?"

After she mentioned her half-siphon, no whip, soy, Venti mocha, she chuckled at herself and thought, What in heaven's name have I done?

She become flushed as the hunky man in the truck pulled to the drive-up window. She looked as Ms. Starbucks asked whether he was open. Furthermore, thereafter, immediately, she looked as he drove away.

Exactly when she got to the window, she learned through Ms. Starbucks' snickers that he was certainly, added, married even.

A portion of the time singles — and every individual on the planet — will go to uncommon lengths and even humiliate themselves to gravitate toward the next orientation.

Why? Is it considering our normal yearning for sex? Is it considered misery? Trouble? Clumsiness? Synthetics? It might be all of the previously mentioned, but the reaction I should focus on is intimacy.

The human yearning for Intimacy, for veneration, drives us to do things that we never figured we would. Nevertheless, why, and what's the importance here? One night over dinner with a buddy, we discussed intimacy and what it infers. She granted an enchanting little articulation to me to assist me with recalling the certified importance of intimacy. "It implies 'in-to-me-see,'" she said. Alright for sure, it's a blending of our heart with another's, so we can "see into" who they genuinely are, and they can "see into" us. Being close incorporates the mixing of our reality with another's, a mixing of spirits, and a sharing of hearts. This is something we overall extensive for considering the way that it's how God made us. We planned to interact.

Authentic intimacy makes us feel alive like we've been found, like someone finally put away an edge to investigate the profundities of our soul and genuinely see us there. Until we experience real intimacy, we will feel dismissed and ignored, like someone is gazing straight through us. Sadly, we can miss the intimacy that can get the news out, when we fate what we figure we should see when we examine their life, heart, character, and soul. Right when this happens, we will endeavor to frame and make them into who we acknowledge they should be. Hence, we are stunned by their extraordinary qualities, and love and intimacy are destroyed.

Perhaps you are pondering the way that you can create a unique interaction. As well as enduring another person the very way that they are, (Note: This doesn't mean enduring any sort of abuse), certified intimacy can begin once you know yourself. Since the significance of intimacy fundamentally connotes "in-to-me-see," how should anyone "see into" you and what your personality is, your anxieties, dreams, assumptions, and needs aside from on the off chance that you know who you unendingly will allow someone prepared? Experiencing certified intimacy begins with being related to your own heart.

In truth, sharing who we are with others is regularly troublesome. All reverence is a bet. I surrender, it will in general be abnormal revealing the most significant bits of ourselves. Luckily, you don't have to do everything at the same time because making intimacy looks like stripping an onion — it can happen fairly at a time while trust is made.

Intimacy by and large means normal shortcomings, responsiveness, and sharing. It is a significant part of the time present front and center, revering associations like connections and friendships. The term is moreover now and again used to suggest sexual affiliations, but intimacy needn't bother with being sexual.

Intimacy can be essential to keeping a sound public action. In case you avoid intimacy, you could wind up separated or in consistent conflict with others. Right, when the sensation of fear toward intimacy disturbs a relationship, couple directing or individual treatment could help.

BUILDING Intimacy IN A RELATIONSHIP

It is possible to Overcome fears of intimacy. A mindful educator can help you with understanding the crucial sentiments driving your fear. They can help you with tending to these feelings and find better approaches to adjusting to them other than detaching yourself.

Now and again mental prosperity issues like avoidant social conditions can similarly add to intimacy issues. Treating these decisions can in like manner offer basic benefits.

Regardless, when neither one of the associates fears intimacy, a couple could anyway encounter trouble opening ward to each other. Going with thoughts could allow you and your accessory to grow closer.

1. **Show limitations**. Getting to truly acknowledge someone is a serious time liability. The trust-building process is a large part of the time a slow one. Intimacy isn't a race.

2. **Start with the straightforward stuff.** Accepting you find it less difficult to talk about the future than the past, then, at that point, begin by sharing your dreams and targets. As trust manufacturers, you could find it less disturbing to talk about the more problematic subjects.

3. **Talk about your prerequisites.** Is it likely that you are someone who needs a lot of time alone to recharge? How oftentimes do you seize the opportunity to have sex? You can thwart a lot of mistakes in case you tell your assistant obviously what you want rather than expecting your desires are "undeniable".

4. **Respect each other's differences.** To be sure, even the most comfortable accessories have their character. You and your accessory don't need to choose all that to love each other.

If you and your partner fight to move closer to each other, there is still an assumption! Couples therapy can help you with building up your correspondence and tackle mixed-up suppositions. It can similarly help each party with overcoming any sensations of fear of intimacy that may be holding them down. There is no shame in tracking down help.

Chapter 3
The Pillars of Intimacy

Emotional Intimacy

Being sincerely close with someone else implies being straightforward with your most Emotional sentiments, fears, and contemplations. It includes having a solid sense of security and not being judged. Also, everything revolves around being no different from the other individual.

Financial Intimacy

Financial intimacy happens when two individuals in a relationship are 100 percent genuine about their convictions toward cash.

Physical Intimacy

In a heartfelt connection, it could incorporate clasping hands, nestling, kissing, and sex. Your relationship doesn't need to be sexual or heartfelt to have physical intimacy.

Spiritual Intimacy

Otherworldly intimacy is the best indicator of one's conjugal intimacy and prosperity from the perspective of Emotional importance. At the point when one's relationship with God makes significance and reason in one's life, it decidedly works on both conjugal intimacy and prosperity.

Recreational Intimacy

Recreational intimacy is the point at which you and your partner find leisure activities or interests that you share as an approach to additional holding and interfacing. At the point when this viewpoint is absent seeing someone, can begin to feel dull. Between the planned operations and funds of life, good times can without much of a stretch get shoved aside.

Sexual Intimacy

At the point when individuals take part in arousing or sexual activity. At the point when individuals utilize "intimacy," they are frequently alluding to this kind. Model: Two darlings participate in foreplay, knowing how each other likes to be touched.

Mental Intimacy

Think about mental intimacy as an accord: It's wonderful, testing, and invigorating. "For certain individuals, this is extraordinary mind and repartee — they love bobbing off one another, testing one another,"

Chapter 4
Emotional Intimacy

Emotional intimacy can be one of the main elements of a relationship. One diary characterized Emotional intimacy as including "an impression of intimacy to another that permits sharing of individual sentiments, joined by assumptions for figuring out, insistence, and exhibitions of mindful."

To develop Emotional intimacy, find the opportunity to pay attention to and share with your partner every day. Likewise, cause notes of unique minutes or things that to help you to remember your partner so you can tell them you're pondering them.

Emotional Intimacy is When individuals have a real sense of reassurance discussing their thoughts with one another, even awkward ones.

Model: A lady trusts her sister about her self-perception issues. She confides in her kin to offer solace as opposed to utilizing her frailties against her.

Emotional intimacy implies developing a feeling of intimacy connecting with how you and your partner feel through compassion, regard, and correspondence. It addresses this sensation of intimacy through the statement of individual, interior sentiments or considerations or convictions, and again seeing those sentiments got, acknowledged, comprehended, and heard by the other party. Thus, assuming you've at any point considered how to be cozy without contact or how to be personal without sex, presently you know.

Emotional intimacy is one of the main kinds to impart to your partner. It implies you're ready to communicate your sentiments and feelings in the relationship, which requires some weakness.

Having the option to impart various feelings to your partner makes trust, which constructs serious areas of

strength for a solid relationship. You can converse with one another about anything, regardless of how troublesome the discussion may be.

Methods for working on emotional intimacy

Cultivating Emotional intimacy is a continuous practice and, in the same way as other things, may get some margin to dominate. In any case, there are a couple of things you can do — beginning this evening — to further develop the Emotional association you have with your partner.

Be decisively powerless to procure their trust
Regardless of whether we've invested a huge measure of energy with somebody, separating our walls is now and again troublesome. However you can't compel one more to become defenseless, you can make a special effort to be weak yourself.

"The act of vital weakness is fundamentally significant. Rather than attempting to be weak in each part of your life, pick one spot to begin," This could mean sharing something that occurred working you probably won't have in any case examined, communicating an inclination

you've had in the past that has been difficult to share, or uncovering a reality about yourself that you've been clutching.

At the point when you interface Emotionally with your partner by communicating your sentiments and sharing your weaknesses, you are encountering personal intimacy. Imparting your most Emotional contemplations and feelings to your partner is, for some couples, one of the most compensating parts of their relationship.

Having Emotional intimacy implies that you will feel near your partner, and sincerely associated and upheld. In a marriage with Emotional intimacy, you can let your watchman down (be powerless), and share with your life partner your feelings of trepidation, expectations, and dreams. At the point when you and your partner are sincerely private, you can be completely yourself.

In a relationship with Emotional distance, you are bound to feel forlorn or angry. You are more averse to feeling trust, love, wellbeing, or backing.

Emotional intimacy isn't equivalent to sexual intimacy. Regardless of how great your sexual encounters are

when Emotional intimacy is missing the relationship will endure. Fortunately, as a team fabricates Emotional intimacy, their sexual coexistence will in general turn out to be seriously fulfilling.

Emotional intimacy isn't equivalent to sexual intimacy. However, it can improve sex.

We want Emotional intimacy. As people, we are designed for association. Emotional intimacy lights up our temperament by initiating feel-great synapses: oxytocin, endorphins, dopamine, and serotonin. Intimacy could expand our future.

Chapter 5

What is financial intimacy and for what reason is it significant? Obviously, a wide range of intimacy in a relationship is significant. Yet, any reasonable person would agree intimacy implies various things to various individuals. A few of us interface intimacy to being more loving. Maybe we could clasp hands or give each other a kiss on the cheek.

Others think relationship intimacy implies drilling down into our most profound sentiments and convictions. What's more, obviously, there's likewise physical intimacy in the room! Yet, Financial intimacy is similarly pretty much as significant as all the above mentioned. And keeping in mind that it may not be top of the psyche, or feel especially heartfelt, financial intimacy is a fundamental part of a relationship.

What does financial intimacy resemble?
At the point when financial intimacy exists, there's ideal concordance between the two partners about the subject of cash. At its ideal, cash gives us an agreeable way of life and the basics we really want. These

incorporate a rooftop over our heads and the food on our plates. Be that as it may, to say the least, cash can be a wellspring of stress, with obligation or the absence of cash destroying our satisfaction.

Financial intimacy happens when two individuals in a relationship are 100 percent legit about their convictions toward cash. Basically, the two partners are in arrangement to make a solid financial relationship with trust at the center.

What happens when Financial similarity doesn't exist?
Tragically, even cheerful couples who have been together for a lifetime aren't monetarily cozy all the time. What's more, a few normal issues crop up when there's an absence of Financial similarity. Look at the accompanying indications.

Mysteries about obligation or betting
44% of Americans maintain cash mysteries from their partner, including those connected with betting compulsion. Privileged insights may be concealing a checking, investment funds, or Visa account from their other half.

Others have an obligation they haven't unveiled to their partner. However, who is this influencing? Research recommends this is an issue that is more normal in twenty to thirty-year-olds than in Gen Xers or children of post-war America.

Financial unevenness
The amount you procure is likewise an enormous issue. At the point when each partner carries an alternate pay to the Financial table, this can make issues with security in a relationship. A few higher workers feel they're sponsoring the way of life of their lower-paid partner. While those on a lower pay might be concerned they're not sufficient for their other half. Financial intimacy may likewise be missing assuming that one partner will in general sprinkle their money more than the other.

This is elevated on the off chance that they're utilizing a shared service to subsidize their spending. The two partners pay into a similar record, yet one is taking more out than the other.

Correspondence breakdowns

It's a well-known fact that cash can cause contentions in connections. As a matter of fact, Financial choices are a regular wellspring of contention between couples who are hitched or living respectively.

Research uncovers that 7 of every 10 Americans couldn't help contradicting their other half about funds in the previous year. What's more, this sort of correspondence breakdown can have adverse results, including the conclusion of the friendship.

Absence of trust

Have you ever known about Financial disloyalty? This happens when one partner lies about cash, frequently out of dread of their partner figuring out reality. It's frequently compared to somebody engaging in extramarital relations because of the data hidden from an partner and the hurt caused.

Be that as it may, how does this influence couples? 41% of Americans guarantee they'd probably cut off their friendship on the off chance that their partner was unscrupulous about their funds. Of these, 20% say the harmed trust would make it very logical they'd throw in the towel.

Step-by-step instructions to have Financial intimacy conversations at various relationship stages

Need to keep away from issues brought about by Financial unfaithfulness and contrariness? The best methodology for couples is to be 100 percent genuine at each phase of the relationship.

While each matching is unique, a few normal topics and conversation focuses crop up en route. Follow these tips to begin.

At the point when you are dating

Simply getting to know one another? This is an extraordinary chance to gain proficiency with somewhat more about the other individual. Pose unobtrusive inquiries to pass judgment on their perspectives about funds.

How does your date esteem cash? Do you have comparative convictions and financial yearnings?

You probably shouldn't ask however many inquiries as your bookkeeper would. All things considered, you're dating so you would rather not put them off! However, you can see whether they're quick to purchase a home and save for what's to come.

Regardless of whether you're not happy posing the inquiries out and out, there might be indications. Pay special attention to signals that your heartfelt premium likes to party hard and blow their money away.

Utilize these initial not many dates to suss out on the off chance that your financial convictions are adjusted. If they're not, this isn't a major issue. However, on the off chance that you can't envision turning out to be monetarily cozy with this individual, later on, the relationship may not merit going after. It's your call!

Moving in together
At the point when things are somewhat more serious, the subsequent stage is frequently to move in together. Furthermore, this is a major cash choice. Regardless of whether you're leasing first as opposed to purchasing, there are a lot of Financial visits to have together.

The most vital move toward Financial intimacy is to plunk down and talk about your cash and the executive's plans. Preferably, this transformation ought to occur before you've formally moved in together.

How might you divide the bills? Will you have a shared service? Will you split the lease 50/50 or each pay an extent in light of your pay rates?

There are no set-in-stone responses here. The point is to have a fair conversation to guarantee you're headed for Financial similarity and that you're OK with the arrangement.

Purchasing a home together

Purchasing a home together is many times the following stage if living respectively has worked out in a good way. This is another enormous step.

Financial intimacy here implies examining how you'll bear the cost of a downpayment on your most memorable home. Will you each save half? Maybe this is preposterous. In which case, will you pick an alternate split given your profit? Additionally consider whose name the property will be in (regularly, this sounds joint). Remember to examine how you'll part the home loan costs. Furthermore, calculate the expense of customary month-to-month charges, and your way to deal with keeping up with the property.

Is it true or not that you are both dedicated to setting aside cash for home fixes and restorative updates? Or on the other hand could one of you rather burn through cash on costly get-aways and status buys like another vehicle?

Therefore it's useful to comprehend an individual's Financial inspirations while you're dating.

Getting hitched
On the off chance that you're recently connected, congrats! This is a thrilling time and another part of everyday life. Having a visit about your finances is likewise an opportunity! Arranging a wedding and vacation can be costly (even though it doesn't necessarily need to be).

Before you go overboard with taking a gander at dresses and scenes, have a straightforward conversation about the amount you intend to go through on your exceptional day. A few couples might be in total agreement about this, others will track down there's a slight jumble.

The expense of your wedding is just a single part of marriage worth being monetarily private about. Before

sealing the deal, you may likewise need to examine the chance of consenting to a pre-matrimonial arrangement if you are both in total agreement around one. A prenuptial understanding or an early understanding is an official agreement. It frames what might befall the property and Financial privileges of every life partner assuming the marriage are close in separate.

Prenups can appear to be unromantic, as they're now centered around the end when the marriage presently can't seem to start.

In any case, where one or the two partners has huge Financial resources, a prenup understanding offers additional security and can be a fundamental piece of a Financial intimacy talk.

Financial intimacy takes collaboration

Are you and your partner expecting to work on your Financial similarity? Know you're in good company! Also, more critically, you don't have to endeavor this objective without help from anyone else.

Various Financial experts are accessible to help your Financial intimacy objectives. In any case, you can likewise teach yourself by taking a Smart Young lady

Money course or by plunging into our enlightening online journal articles.

Experts are accessible to address contingent upon your relationship stage and your particular worries. For instance, you could address a Financial consultant, bookkeeper, contract counselor, or expense guide. What's more, you can look for direction independently or as a couple. One way or the other, this will guarantee each partner has all the data they need, made sense of by an expert. From here, you can get back to your relationship as equivalents with an arrangement set up to handle your funds together.

Accomplishing Financial intimacy is rarely past the point of no return
Anything that relationship stage you're at, Financial intimacy merits accomplishing. Furthermore, this is an objective reachable. Start by opening up to your partner about any worries you have. Then, gauge their heartbeat about turning out to be all the more monetarily viable.

Regardless of whether Financial intimacy has been inadequate with regards to, refocusing is rarely past the point of no return. Start with a transparent conversation about how you both view cash.

From here, you'll make joint Financial objectives together. Furthermore, remember to look for proficient counsel to assist you with keeping focused.

Chapter 6

Physical Intimacy

While an embrace or holding a hand are the two instances of physical intimacy, this type is most normally utilized concerning sex. And keeping in mind that sex is significant seeing someone, you can likewise show physical intimacy through kissing, clasping hands, nestling, and skin-to-skin contact.

While these little physical shows of friendship might appear to be ordinary, they can assist you and you're cooperating with developing a sensation of intimacy. Physical intimacy alludes to body intimacy. It can include embracing, snuggling, kissing, and clasping hands, contingent upon the idea of the relationship.

However, physical intimacy isn't restrictive to better halves. Guardians and kids and even companions can foster non-sexual physical intimacy.

This sort of intimacy includes safe touch and vicinity that can upgrade sensations of profound intimacy. Honestly, physical intimacy isn't significant, in light of the fact that it's the structure generally famously connected with the term.

"Physical intimacy is basically about unwinding into it, participating in the progression of it, getting into the occasion, and sharing, giving, getting, and communicating what feels better. Everything revolves around the association, energy, the giving and getting of delight, and intimacy,"

Physical intimacy
Physical intimacy incorporates both sexy and sexual movement ordinarily between two people and the sharing of responses, contemplations, and feelings that are associated with these exercises.

In reality, physical intimacy incorporates an extensive variety of conduct. All that from hand-holding to the entire day of love-production. It incorporates a wide scope of physical contact, for example,

foreplay or non-coital sexual action
washing together
swimming together
pleasuring

stroking each other's body
sex
the luminosity (e.g., the delicate words that are traded
after sexual movement)

Likely Obstructions to Physical intimacy
Physical intimacy is some of the time hard to create and
now and again, boundaries might arise:

One of the fundamental hindrances is the thin spotlight
that the vast majority put on their conduct around here.
For the most part, individuals will generally zero in on sex
as though it were the main articulation of erotic or sexual
inclinations toward someone else. On the off chance that
reality, continuing too quickly to and through sex is one
of the significant objections numerous ladies have about
their physical personal connections with their partners.

One more obstruction to the agreeable articulation of
physical intimacy happens when one disregards one's
apprehensiveness about a specific action or the
practicality of a specific way of behaving.
Apprehensiveness overlooked can deliver sexual
hindrances, blocks, and mood killers. One of the

wellsprings of apprehensiveness might be the trepidation that is engaged with physical intimacy.

Fears that might be associated with physical intimacy:

One trepidation is the feeling of dread toward being contacted. A few people are not extremely familiar with being contacted, being stroked, to being OK with material feeling.

There may be the feeling of dread toward breaking a no. There are various restrictions in many societies connected with physical intimacy. In any event, when an individual is hitched, it is frequently challenging to switch off the impact of a portion of these restrictions with which they have lived before marriage.

There is the apprehension about failing to keep a grip on oneself, of forsaking oneself for physical happiness. Physical intimacy much of the time includes surrendering control - giving up, and for an apprehensive individual of letting completely go, this can be a restless circumstance.

Many individuals dread pregnancy because of physical intimacy. Albeit prophylactic data and conception

prevention procedures are promptly accessible, individuals hold fears about pregnancy, maybe from data or fantasies that come from youth or puberty. These apprehensions can impede feeling good in a truly close connection.

There is the feeling of dread toward physically communicated sickness (sexually transmitted diseases), which much of the time is a sensible trepidation especially if both of the partners have participated in sexual activity with different partners and if both of the partners aren't rehearsing safe sex methods.

There is apprehension about responsibility or judgment either from peers, relatives or at times from the congregation.

For some individuals, physical intimacy is an original encounter. For an individual procedure into a genuinely personal connection, there are numerous new things to encounter. In the event that an individual is troubled about clever encounters, the trepidation related to novel encounters will make boundaries to physical intimacy.

Ways Of conquering Snags to Physical intimacy
One of the central things an individual can do is to take things at their own rate - a rate with which the person is agreeable.

It means a lot to allow oneself to say "no" when "no" is the right solution for you; and on the other hand, to allow yourself to say "OK" when "yes" is the right response and be willing to get a sense of ownership with the outcomes of those choices and activities. At the point when these yes and no responses come from one's very own arrangement of values, one's solace with physical intimacy increments.

Become mindful of one's trepidation and what might be delivering the apprehensiveness about physical intimacy. When trepidation is recognized, one can work with it.

Chapter 7

Spiritual Intimacy

Spiritual intimacy implies feeling close, approved, and safe sharing your deepest thoughts and convictions on life's motivation and your association with divine energies.

It's as yet an obscured idea since it might mean various things to various individuals. It doesn't be guaranteed to mean the two individuals have similar convictions, however, it might include sharing a more extensive idea of otherworldliness. For instance, you may both accept that you should be loyal and legit in everything you do, regardless of whether you have a place with various religions.

Sharing this higher feeling of direction might foster a private intimacy that permits you to project a coexistence, for example.

Spiritual intimacy doesn't be guaranteed to need to revolve around religion. Basically, talking about the more profound significance of life implies being capable. It can unquestionably include religion, however, regardless of

anything else, you're ready to discuss your profound convictions without being judged. Spiritual intimacy doesn't mean your viewpoints and convictions need to coordinate — it implies you're willing to regard and value them come what may.

While you won't be guaranteed to need to encounter a wide range of intimacy, it's essential to comprehend that they're undeniably interlaced to make areas of strength for a relationship. For instance, having sexual intimacy without feeling associated with other, non-sexual levels is difficult.

Simple Methods TO Assemble Spiritual Intimacy WITH YOUR Partner
Spirituality is a significant part of one's life. Developing in a spiritual sense with your partner can be an extraordinary encounter on the off chance that you consider and execute these 5 simple methods to fabricate spiritual intimacy. If you have any desire to

encounter a profound intimacy that resembles no other this is an ideal article for you.

#1. Tolerating Your Partner for What Their identity is

Comprehend that you and your partner might be at various stages in your spiritual excursion. This won't cause struggle on the off chance that you don't permit it to. Your partner might choose to venerate in a manner that is not the same as the manner in which you choose to revere. All the more critically, you ought to attempt to be available to new things as it connects with love and dedication. Having a receptive outlook will you're your excursion to spiritual intimacy more pleasant.

#2. Figure out how to Compromise

Comprehend that your partner probably shouldn't go to chapel or go to the Book of scriptures concentrate as frequently as you would like or the other way around. This shouldn't end your excursion to accomplishing spiritual intimacy. Track down imaginative ways of remembering your partner for your love. Associate in a profound sense with your life partner such that functions admirably for themselves and for you. Set practical assumptions and figure out how to think twice about. Church each Sunday might work for you yet not so much for them.

#3. Commit the Time

Comprehend that building spiritual intimacy can take time. Giving chance to love as a unit will end up being valuable and assist you with holding with your partner on a spiritual level. Make certain to commit a particular time all through the week to keep an eye on your spirituality with your partner. Whether it will be church each Sunday, going to Book of scriptures study, imploring together, or just perusing the Holy book to each other. Commit time to draw nearer in a profound way.

#4. Figure out Your Partner's Qualities

To comprehend your partner means to comprehend their convictions and the things they esteem the most (for example family time, genuineness, going to chapel consistently). This understanding will consider you and your partner to develop nearer and construct a strong bond. This will consider you to truly realize your partner's thought process is significant and what those convictions will mean for your relationship. You ought to be aware on the off chance that your partner isn't enthusiastic about spirituality and they ought to know how you feel about your spirituality. Having the right discussion will let you know where you are on your excursion and how you can meet your mate mostly on this excursion.

#5. Welcome Your Spirituality into Your Relationship

At the point when you and your partner end up in a struggle with each other, worrying about funds, or in a terrible spot in everyday welcome your spirituality to comfort you. Permit your partner to take part in this safe place with you. At the point when there are issues that all of you apparently can't tackle, go to your spiritual convictions with your partner. Permit your spiritual convictions to direct you in your relationship. Permit your common convictions to assist you to settle on your choices with your partner. Welcome your otherworldliness into your conditions.

I trust these 5 simple methods to construct spiritual intimacy with your partner to assist you and your partner with having an extraordinary relationship.

Chapter 8

Recreational Intimacy

At the point when individuals bond during recreation exercises. Individuals may "sync up" their activities in collaboration or end up acting as one. recreational intimacy implies finding leisure activities and interests you can encounter together! Normal interests keep you feeling associated, particularly when the dullness of regular daily existence kicks in. The objective of recreational intimacy is to keep the flash alive in your relationship. Have a good time together! While it's as yet essential to have separate interests and indeed, you ought to in any case try to do things together to assist with keeping you feeling associated.

Recreational Intimacy is doing things together. This is one of those areas in a relationship where couples put a great deal of time and exertion into when they are dating yet frequently disregard it once they get hitched. Heading to sleep and awakening together has some way or another persuaded many couples that they are getting bunches of "together" time and needn't bother to be deliberate any longer. Recreational intimacy is about something beyond being available in a similar area, it's tied in with making recollections, venturing into one another's reality, and playing together. Instances of Sporting Intimacy may be:

Going for a stroll or working out together

Going to a show or game

Playing a prepackaged game or game together

Going out to eat or for espresso and pastry

The objective of this time together is to have a good time without examining the business side of marriage, areas of contention, or subjects that have the capability of being hostile. Most couples do that enough as of now. Season of recreational Intimacy ought to be calm and cheerful.

Chapter 9

Sexual Intimacy

As the most unmistakable, this sort of intimacy is for the most part clear as crystal. All things considered, it's something other than having intercourse! Sexual intimacy is additionally about sharing dreams, wants, and needs. At last, it makes a place of refuge to open dependent upon one another about what you like and could do without being unafraid of being judged or closed out.

When you're ready to serenely discuss your sexual necessities with one another, you've arrived at the most elevated level of sexual intimacy. This incorporates making and regarding solid limits. Besides the fact that this works on actual intimacy, however further develops trust and correspondence also.

Sexual intimacy in marriage is vital to the strength and solidarity between you and your accomplice; nonetheless, sexual intimacy includes considerably more than sex alone. The intimacy divided between you and your accomplice has included the certifiable intimacy, backing, and friendship you share.

Sexual intimacy is likewise the common feeling of solace you feel in being your actual self and offering your viewpoints, sentiments, and wants to each other. Although sex is significant in sexual intimacy, it is absolutely by all accounts not the only part nor is it the essential variable. If it was, any two individuals who share a sexual experience would, as a matter of course, have sexual intimacy, and this isn't true. Not even love implies that you will have sexual intimacy. Many couples might adore one another, yet miss the mark on essential intimacy. Growing valid and enduring sexual intimacy takes work and a craving between the two accomplices to focus on a delightful and excellent relationship.

Beneath we will examine a few justifications for why you and your accomplice ought to investigate and reinforce your sexual intimacy for a sound and blissful marriage. Sexual intimacy keeps you both actually and sincerely sound. Investigations have discovered that individuals who are hitched are not more joyful, however on the off chance that the connection between the couple is sound and fulfilling, wedded individuals improve wellbeing.

Sexual intimacy in marriage implies that you will want to oversee life stressors or any significant life-altering events all the more realistic and support each other all the while. Sexual intimacy can help your marriage on the off chance that you are attempting to concur or get along in different regions. For certain couples, sexual intimacy holds the marriage together during turbulent times or times of strain in the relationship.

Sexual intimacy advances sound confidence. Your confidence should get from your convictions about yourself and your self-esteem, yet it most certainly helps when your accomplice is steady and glad for you and your achievements.

Sexual intimacy will help you in different aspects of your life. Your vocation, your abilities to nurture, and your kinships will be better when you have a sound, close connection with your accomplice.

Chapter 10

Mental Intimacy

Think about mental intimacy as an agreement: It's delightful, testing, and invigorating. At the point when individuals feel happy with imparting thoughts and insights, in any event, when they conflict.

Model: Two companions banter about the significance of life. They appreciate getting each other's thoughts and don't want to "win" the contention.

Mental intimacy alludes to sharing your thoughts, assessments, and life points of view. It might likewise include mentally testing one another and being available to learn, or possibly taking into account, the other individual's thoughts.

Having invigorating conversations about various subjects and having a protected outlook on communicating your own perspectives is important for mental intimacy.

The key is to extend shared regard, in any event, when you have a contrasting perspective.

The general advantage of scholarly intimacy is having the option to impart considerations and insights that are regarded by your accomplice. It tends to be essentially as straightforward as examining a book or having more dubious discussions about legislative issues or religion. Regardless of the conversation, you stay receptive when you have various perspectives or suppositions.

Similar to emotional intimacy, mental intimacy requires a weakness. It considers a place of refuge to discuss intense points without being put down or scorned.

Chapter 11

Each Pillar Matters

Intimacy is a significant element of blissful and solid marriage. On the off chance that you are not quite as personal as you used to be, is it a reason to worry? Absence of intimacy in marriage influences surprisingly couples. While the reasons fluctuate, the people who are in this present circumstance are interested to be aware on the off chance that a relationship can endure this or not.

What Causes Absence of Intimacy in a Marriage?
Might it be said that you are in a sexless marriage? There are a couple of normal justifications for why couples foster an absence of intimacy.

Stress is the most widely recognized reason. Stress can emerge out of different sources, for example, tension from work, youngster care, and monetary difficulties in the family. There are a few examinations that show the connection between stress and a diminishing sex drive.

The disdain in a marriage is another component that can prompt an absence of intimacy among wedded couples.

If there are irritating issues in your marriage, it can make a mate pull away and become genuinely far off. Making distance can likewise cause diminished profound intimacy. At the point when there is no emotional association, actual intimacy endures as well.

At long last, dismissal is one more justification for why there is no intimacy in your marriage. On the off chance that you dismissed your companion's advances previously, this can influence their confidence as it causes them to feel undesirable and ugly.

Absence of Intimacy in a Marriage: What You Should Be Aware
A marriage needs a negligible degree of intimacy to get by. There are a couple of things you want to be aware of to assist you with adapting to an absence of intimacy in your marriage.

1. **IT IS Normal TO HAVE LESS SEX WHEN Hitched.**
A study report named "The Social Association of Sexuality" distributed in 1994 (and is as yet important today), reports that up to 20% of hitched couples see a decrease in the recurrence of sex in their relationship.

Subsequently, on the off chance that you see a drop in the intimacy level in your marriage, you are in good company. There are a few factors that can add to this, such as monetary battles, medical problems, psychological well-being issues, and some more. Assuming you have kids, dealing with them can go through your energy and leave minimal left for private experiences with your life partner.

There could be different issues inside the marriage that can prompt a sexless relationship. Anything the reason is, you want to decide it so you can do whatever it takes to resuscitate intimacy.

2. **Intimacy IN A MARRIAGE Isn't JUST ABOUT SEX.**
Sex isn't the best way to communicate intimacy in a marriage. Physical and profound intimacy should remain inseparable.

Emotional intimacy is how you express your friendship towards your mate. This can be a knowing look from across the room or how you grin when you see him/her toward the finish of the functioning day. That emotional association that you have for one another can be an extremely personal thing that you share.

Physical intimacy, then again, isn't just about sex. It could likewise be kissing, embracing, nestling, and clasping hands. All types of communication intimacy are critical to set your marriage.

3. Relationships NEED Intimacy TO Make due.
Intimacy is a significant part to cause a union to flourish and get by. The level and sort of intimacy will contrast starting with one couple and then onto the next. A few couples like intimacy while others can make do without it.

The issue of an absence of intimacy in a marriage possibly emerges when the two individuals differ about how significant intimacy is to every one of them. It is fundamental to transparently talk about intimacy in your union with the guarantee that your necessities are met.

4. A SEXLESS MARRIAGE CAN Get by.
Sex is one of the most basic signs of intimacy in a marriage, which is the reason it is a significant point to examine too. Married couples can be cheerful in their relationship even without sex, particularly when they esteem one another and show regard. Furthermore, there are alternate ways of compensating for the

absence of sex in the marriage, for example, doing things together that you appreciate. A few couples like to travel together, take part in their number one side interests, etc. These exercises can be similarly essentially as private as sex.

Now and again, sexless relationships occur because of reasons unchangeable as far as the couple might be concerned, for example, medical issues or maturing. These couples have figured out how to acknowledge the way that sex is never again part of their marriage and track down alternate ways of communicating their adoration for one another.

5. **A few Relationships Will does not Make do WITHOUT Intimacy.**
While sexless relationships work for some, they won't work for all. Truth be told, the absence of sex can offset some other positive parts of their marriage. Subsequently, numerous connections end because of an absence of intimacy.

This possibly turns into an issue when the two players are not in concurrence with the kind and measure of intimacy they need. For instance, one mate values actual intimacy (like sex) however different doesn't believe it's as significant. You can't drive somebody to change their view about intimacy since it must be something they normally care about.

At the point when there is no arrangement between the two parties regarding their perspective on intimacy, one of the gatherings cuts off despondent in the friendship. At the point when this occurs, the couple can discuss how they can arrive at a split of the difference. A ton of couples go through guidance to adapt to intimacy issues. A few people will deal with expanding intimacy in their marriage. Be that as it may, on the off chance that one party doesn't display ability, then it probably won't end up working.

The Reality

On the off chance that you need to live in a more joyful, better marriage, it is vital to resolve issues like an absence of intimacy in a marriage. This is only one part of your marriage however a vital one. Work on further developing intimacy in your relationship to fortify your emotional and physical bond.